The Fat Lady
Struck Dumb

David Waltner-Toews

The Fat Lady Struck Dumb

Brick Books

Canadian Cataloguing in Publication Data

Waltner-Toews, David, 1948 –
   The fat lady struck dumb

Poems.
ISBN 1-894078-12-8

I. Title.

PS8595.A61F37 2000   C811'.54   C00-932568-9
PR9199.3.W34F37 2000

We acknowledge the support of the Canada Council for the Arts
for our publishing programme. The support of the Ontario Arts
Council is also gratefully acknowledged.

Photo on the cover is of a dog being celebrated in Kathmandu,
taken by Dider Chemin.
Author photo credit: Matthew Waltner-Toews

This book is set in Janson Text and Novarese.

Design and layout by Alan Siu.

Printed and bound by Sunville Printco Inc.

Brick Books
431 Boler Road, Box 20081
London, Ontario N6K 4G6
brick.books@sympatico.ca

To Kathy,
for more than a quarter century of
love and friendship

Table of Contents

This I know at great cost:
All life is not outward,
Nor is all death from within.

Pablo Neruda, "The Traveller"

I.

A Post-Cambrian Lament

Death of a Humanist

In the chapel of La Faloria convent,
Cortina, Italy, I meditate
in the quiet dawn,
a shadow of habits
supplicating behind me,
before me the silhouette of a cross,
stark against the white mountain
and the Arian clear blue sky.

Later, I climb
a well-groomed mountain path
through the congregation of trees.
At the top there is a chapel, a guest house,
and a large military gun.
Up there, the sheer delight
of earth's power, barely constrained,
rolls like an organ fugue
down, away from me
into a complex canon of trills and rocks
and breath-taking valleys,
up, billowing like a ragged wind-blown sheet
into the vaulted skies.
It tugs, at every peak,
against the slipping grip
of guest house, chapel, gun.

Below, in Milan,
I walk the narrow streets,
feeling at home, pause in the courtyard
of the Giuseppe Verdi Music Conservatory
in the Chiesa della Passione (AD 1486).
Violin sounds dip and wing
from balconies,
musicians in formal attire
pace gracefully, humming.
Around a corner, the Duomo
rises in the Central Plaza,
from a distance like an intricate

wet-dripped sand castle.
Up close, it is a rock-heap
of men on horses, torsos rippling,
biceps bulging in triumph and misery,
swords, flags, crosses
up-thrust in victory.

For a millennium these bodies
chopped, hauled, re-organized,
re-shaped wood, stone, earth,
cut and slashed each other over differences
of opinion, convinced each other
with argument, praised God, made
God redundant with thumbscrews,
racks, irons, stakes,
proved that people were superior
to God in all these things, carved the Duomo
in stone dragged down from the Dolomites,
re-built the mountains
in our own image until wild snow,
rock canyons, fearsome beast,
were transformed to cathedral, sewer, hospital,
factory, guest house, gun.

I sit at the edge of the plaza,
security helicopters buzzing overhead,
brilliant lights enflaming the magnificence
of stone, eating pizza, drinking red wine.
I sense the full weight of it,
the mass of flesh screaming
through the centuries, raining
down on me, arms, legs,
bodies of knowledge,
corporate legacies
like a legion of mad prions re-making the earth
in our image, demanding rights, attention, liberty,
trampling every living thing in the pursuit

of truth, beauty,
and efficient management.

I close my eyes,
recalling the small, dusky space
where Leonardo depicted a gathering of twelve men
arguing during a meal, one,
lost in sadness, seeing too far ahead.
I imagine the possibility of unprovoked, unexplained
acts of wildness and love,
animals escaping, unfinished business,
finished business undone, half-fallen cathedrals
a-whirr with the happy chat and clicks
of swallows and bats, and
scattered showers of light.

Something brushes my cheek
in the dark, gently,
a small, dry, green hand,
the touch of a wild and fragile thought, lost in the midst
of all this order, like a friend, remembered,
reaching out from between the cracks
in an aqueduct, or a cathedral,
touching to reach me.

I open my eyes.
A wind sweeps across the plaza,
the lights go out,
unsure lovers huddle slowly past.

I feel something
like hope. I hold it gently,
feel it scrabble and nip
in the chambers of my heart,
like a small bird, or a mouse caught
in the garden shed.

I let it go free in the dusk.

Death of a Naturalist

In the red-hued water
off Pugwash, Nova Scotia,
red jelly-coloured jellyfish
slip and waltz one over the other
to the shore. In the retreating tide
they sag into tangles of crocheted
seaweed, like fatigued dancers
into satin bedsheets.

What wild, colossal waste!
What brutish inefficiency!
What waves of beautiful recycling
tumbling over under one form to another
life unfolding rolling folding from sighing choirs
of plankton to waltzing fish to jitterbugging microbes
to clams with laid-back erections
pushing up through the muck at my feet
to garlicked succulence in oil
to me. What would I feel
if the sea were casting human babies
up on the sand?
What do my feelings matter?

Out on the bay, a Right Whale and a Humpback
break the static-hiss of waves.
In clear, dark lines, they
graze the interface of vast unspeaking worlds,
raise cryptic messages,
slip under.
Waves of shore birds lift, turn and fall
like a grand musical score.
The rising sea laps at my toes,
sucks at my heels.

Somewhere inland, an aging porcupine
bids his friends a calm farewell.
Around them, choirs of flies hum distractedly;

the crows cannot restrain
their raucous glee.

I am retreating homeward, inland,
drawn by the pistons' fevered beat
through falling night, away
from nature's dark and brilliant
orchestration, drawn to four walls, a quilted bed,
my lover's arms, high-minded dreams
of some sad planet
where every death is wasted,
where life does not require its end
to live again, where passion has no price,
(such thin, immortal poverty of soul!)

where I could turn, relieved, from these, our sacrifice –
the street kids hassling me in Kathmandu
and Kenya, the girls bent over,
beating waves of cotton on the rocks in India
and Peru, the peasant farmers in Honduras
scratching chicken feed from mountain soil,
from spirits broken,
from hearts undone.

The porcupine waits on the road
raising, with slow dignity,
in the glare of inexorable lights,
his quivering crown. The driver
flinches
at the thump, but does not stop.

All night outside our cabin
the sea-tongues sing
of love and death,
of jellyfish and fishermen,
of whales and sailing watchers,
of diatoms, mud shrimp, sandpipers,
old porcupines, middle-aged poets

laundry girls, street kids, farmers, coiling and recoiling,
arias, duets, and chorus after rich-voiced
chorus, echoing against sea-glass and sand
against shifting fossil-bearing shale.

As morning fog inexorably
brightens
in the harbour, I turn
to face the window
and drift
to sleep.

The Dogs of Kathmandu

As moss cloaks crumbling
rust-red bricks with luminescent green,
so dogs in Kathmandu
restore the fractured kinship lines
among the city's broken lives.

At dusk they weave a snuffling web
among the children begging,
or at play with marbles,
vendors of rice and guava,
ripe tomatoes and fish,
an old Gurkha dozing
by his door, orange and azure
women testing cloth, me
in a pink cotton shirt,
a bargain in Canada,
– made in Nepal–
and, in my pocket,
a ticket, I think, home.

By night announcing dawn, thieves,
foreigners, or mates in heat,
the broken dreams of rhinos or snow leopards,
by day the dogs will eat and sleep,
guarding the shadows
of Ganesh and Vishnu.

In chill pre-dawn they stretch
and defecate. Old women
follow them
with broken brooms.

A Man Sits Naked

A man sits naked
on a mountain
in the fog.
He feels the cool breath
of nature on his skin, the clean
press of rock against his bum.
He feels solidarity
with his species, at one
with all living things
back into the ancient mists before time,
back to slimy things climbing
through algae and *equisetum*
up the shore to earth, stones, roots.
He comes down
with stress-induced pulmonary infection.
He learns about the laws of Nature.

A man sits naked
on a street corner
in the sunlight.
He feels a crowd of eager eyes
scanning his body.
He feels the palms of the law
on his buttocks.
He is taken down
for questioning, fined for mischief,
put behind bars. He feels solidarity
with immigrants the world over,
at one with barefoot peasants
displaced from their lands, herded
among bent palms, through fevered marshes
to the edge of the menacing sea.
He learns about the laws of Culture.

A man puts on his clothes.
They let him out of jail.
He climbs a mountain.
He sits on a rock
in bright cold morning light.
He remembers a man
stepping from a boat into the surf,
waves sucking at his cuffs.
He recalls a fragile newborn baby,
held in his chapped hands.
He hears the gulls,
scudding down the wind-waves

crying, crying, crying.

Mt. St Hilaire, walking at night

Clambering over roots, rocks,
crackling branches, brash as humans
in the moon-mottled black fall woods,
I stub my toe, and pitch
silently over the cliff,
somersault through moonlight
and shadow, tumbling tongue-tied
until a sudden explosion
of spores from the leaf bed
announces my arrival. I am on my back,
stunned by fear and beauty.
Chipmunks venture near,
at the edge of my vision,
assessing my value as a source
of peanuts or fragments of bread.
The earth fingers my hair,
tests the flesh of my thighs,
as a woman in the market feels
the ripeness of a peach.

The lung-shock-cold air sighs away from me,
sparkling with stars like wisps of dry snow
drifting across the night sky.
I lie here, remembering nothing.
The sponge of humus
presses wetly through my shirt,
the tiny sprouts and crawlers
pushing through the sulci of my brain,
nosing past my tongue,
speaking of something rotting and brown
in the long night of my being,
laughing, as with a child's careless voice,
for no reason, of purple florets
and bright yellow mushrooms.

A Post-Cambrian Lament

Her feet sting
on the hot Namibian sand.
Far below, now cast in stone,
Cambrian worms once danced, engorged,
the spiny slug fantastique,
carnivorous exuberance ... *Ottoia,*
Hallucigenia, Wiwaxia, Aysheaia ...
limbs and tongues commingled
in a slice of time,
540 million years ago,
ten million wide.

Later, the Bushmen
brushed carefully their scenes of game,
their hunger,
and our insatiable desire
against these rocks:
the graceful leap of creatures
from veldt to stone to wavering
thin air.

From a multiplicity of shapes in species
to this polyphony of human voice:
film-maker, archaeologist, farmer,
cacophonic symphony
of ecotourists, businessmen,
choir of utter poverty.

She stands still at the rim;
the valley falls away
before her.

This is the world's first breath,
its last breath, bated.
From the plunging sweep
below, a shimmering sigh of microbes
lifts, in expectation of great carnage,

an orgy feast across the landscape,
another brilliant efflorescence.

Her limbs strain, quivering slightly,
rooted, mesmerized by sand in wind,
a vision of our end
in hot reflected sun.

A Bill from the Power Company

It begins in New Guinea
with veneration of our ancestors.
It begins with love of wisdom and intelligence.
It begins with admiring the dead,
It begins with our cleverness
and our envy.
It begins with eating the brains
of those whom we admire,
with women and children first.
It ends with Kuru, a spongy Jacuzzi
of laid back prions, engulfing the brain.
It ends with a young woman
throwing herself into the fire.

It begins in America with a dust bowl,
with the world war's devastation.
It begins with hungry children
in Europe and Africa.
It begins with our cleverness
and our lust for power and our tractors.
It begins with cows coming in from the green
wilderness in droves.
It begins with praise of hamburgers
on every tongue.
It begins with some spare change
after shopping for food,
and the thrill of a new car.
It begins with recycling, with efficiency,
with cow-eat-cow.
It ends with old men
hungry for power.
It ends with a mob of mad cows
fed to power stations,
shimmering up in smoke
from the incinerators.

It begins with love of life.
It begins in a white coat.

It begins with cutting and sewing.
It begins with new drugs.
It begins with our cleverness
and our fear of death.
It begins with ingesting those
who have what we want.
It begins with blood transfusions,
with hearts, kidneys, and corneal transplants,
with bone marrow and *dura mater*.
It ends with rabies, with AIDS,
with a slow toppling of prions
across the brain.
It ends with a young man,
unable to walk, unable to speak
his own name.

It begins with flowers and wine.
It begins with clever conversation.
It begins with the love of children,
of making them, and, surprisingly, caring for them.
It begins with a house and a car
and a school and a computer.
It ends with paying
the power bill.
It comes round
to huddling by a campfire
playing old guitars,
singing plaintive melodies,
and, in the ash-black darkness at our backs,
the sound of cows or bears foraging,
and the slow sigh of a rising moon.

My Mother's Heart Attack

Just a touch of the flu,
she told her sister,
sucking back the pain and nausea.
She carried her bags to the plane.
I should home be going
to get some rest,
she said, dabbing the perspiration
from her brow.

When my mother had a heart attack
the sidewalk dropped away behind me,
a huge, creeping crater,
deeper than the Manitoba gravel pits
where teenagers disappeared without a trace
into the blue water.
I had to keep walking, then,
straining not to run,
knowing the cement was crumbling
after me.

The pit can smell your fear.
If you consider fleeing
it will make a sudden, leaping bite
and pull you down.
Like a Blue Heeler,
it is just moving you along.
It knows where you must go.

My mother has seen it all,
from the Czar to Stalin,
Manning and Vanderzalm –
it's all the same.
Your husband dies.
Your children grow up.
Floods and famines,
politicians, families,

accountants, visionaries:
there is nothing new under the sun.

I just keep walking.
I am starting to hear voices,
from the pit, maybe,
or just in my head.
I do not recognize them.
I fear they might be
Haida, Ainu, a Tibetan minority
forgotten even by the Tibetans, an inchoate chorus
of impending extinctions,
clamouring for a mouth.

All I can think of is my mother,
her silence, my tongue.
Under a supple, radiant, red-gold maple tree,
I stop, transfixed,
my heart ringing into my ears.
I ignore the wet nose sniffing
at my heel,
puzzled at how, under the operatic flare
of this mad October sun,
the twisted syntax
of my mother tongue
now from my lips is falling.

On the Death of a Father

When the shadow passes,
you quiver like a small,
hairless mouse, and freeze.
The talons sting
more deeply in the heart
than you expected.
The breathless flight
so far above the happy
trees, house, friends
you barely recognize,
seems forever.

You are left
alone
at the bottom of the sky,
at your doorstep.
At the foot of the stairs
you see him, turning.
He smiles.

When you return
to the kitchen there are someone's children,
a strange, tall man,
cereal in a dish, the telephone
ringing. You cannot remember
what you were doing
before the news. You
run into the street,
looking for signs of familiarity.
When the postman arrives
you hug him, fiercely,
until he pushes you away.

There are no letters.
There is no word.
A phrase turns over and over
in the unutterable darkness

within you.
You search the sky for a shadow
of meaning. You search the faces
of the family standing in your door;
they are waiting, even the cat
between their legs, for a sign.

This sentence is for life.
It will end with a question mark,
or an exclamation;
this cannot be predicted
from the subject or the verb,
from your vague smile,
the giddy rising of your heart from the depths,
or the knife-sharp bends as part of you comes
out of solution.

There is no pause.
You are already in the kitchen
peeling carrots
for lunch.

Here, Not Here

David Porter is all – muscles, heart, mind – all there
in the predatory bite of the February air;

skiing among shadows
on the rolling snow,

winter's jaws fall loose and warm,
the buttery sun charming

him into green and rocky
water-falling thoughts,

winter to spring, a fallen
log, at dusk an aching head; he sprawls

across the quilted bed. Outside the door
Bobbi is fussing at the counter:

apples, tea, cheese, buns;
an aneurism bursts like the sun.

David cannot lie still, must now ski
through these sun-flaming trees

away from this cross country, where
lengthening shadows out behind the deck

crumple like trees into the wreck
of dogs, asleep, this empty chair,

this apple red as cheeks, sun-yellow cheese,
this crust, this cup of still, cold tea.

Mine Field

This is the real me, all mine.

Come inside,
I'll show you my orchids,
teak and palms, wide-eyed
rodents

with whiskery noses,
mountains rising up, snakes
draped
from branches; think of me

as a print: Rousseau or Gauguin.
We can share this peaceable
jungle, if you like;
I can bring you to a small clearing
where petals brush your cheek,
and your knee buckles unexpectedly
from the predator's teeth in your heel.

We can lie down
on a futon of leaves.
Something clicks softly,
like a small steel mouse.

The earth moves.

Absence in Old Quebec

Your absence is a candle, the swish
of curtains, satin-cool hiss of faint

sad clouds along ramparts,
moonlight whispering through rain.

You enter me, sun-tongue, a slim white fish,
slip between sulci, silvery – gone.

In dreams I am a flute your lips caress.

I waken empty, air-song through hollow bone.

Sunday Morning

Crow stands beside the highway,
a priest in black satin
casting his censorious beak
this way and that
under a heavenly crown
of radiant autumn trees.

It is only a matter of time
before a feast, served on God's silver
splatter, comes to his cocky lordship:
a fat squirrel, a tail-wagging dog,
maybe a toddler in overalls,
an old woman with a shawl
a man escaping voices in a car.

I pass Crow on my way to church.
We shall sing in four parts, full force,
at the tops of our lungs,
voices from the past breaching,
at long last, these damned bodies,
carrying our souls with them,
releasing them
in a furious tide of glory.

But this morning, the pianist has a mind of her own.
She wants to transform us
into instruments for her glory.
Her fingers thrum over the ivory ribs,
creating her own bone-rattling
disharmonies, voices to haunt
this patriarchal wilderness we share.
Just when our singing is about to peak,
she leaves us dangling
from a trembling clef.

She knows that all the bad things
in her life were because
she was a woman

and all the bad things
that happened to me
were well-deserved.
She knows, knowing myself,
I will concur.

The woman at the pulpit,
black hair spread back
like raven's wings
fixes her eyes on me.
She speaks of bodies and boundaries,
the body of Christ,
the consummating heat of God.
She has me on my back over the lectern.
Rising white, glistening, luminous and erect
above me, her penetrating insights
reduce me to moans and quivers.

And I am lifted up
into a brave new heaven,
above, finally,
all that history, all those cocky victories
returning now to haunt me,
all those souls rescued from their bodies,
all those rescued bodies, to save our souls,
the children saved at birth,
saved from their better selves,
saved into this war zone, this songless desert,
these chronic poetry shortages,
line-ups for a scrap of humour,
and the long silent night
surrounding us:
this is how the world ends.

This is how the world should end:
a small act of kindness
at the moment I close my eyes,

consumed among the cords of flaming
Wesleyan choruses,

a gentle hand somewhere on my body
a cool, indifferent sun glancing through the car window,
Crow in the rear-view mirror
anxiously waiting by the empty highway.

How the Earth Loves You

One day, perhaps when you are
in your forties, he is at your door
with a spring of daffodils.
Another day he bears lilies,
or jack-in-the-pulpits,
every day a flutter of fresh petals
and another scent whispering
at the skirt of your hair.
He seems disconcertingly traditional.
He brings roses, for instance, red ones.
You are bemused.
You look past him, sheepishly,
to the shapes of clouds,
to the paling blue sky.
When your eyes return from flight
you see your hand is bleeding,
you are clutching a sprig of thorns,
and he is gone.

He returns with fat red tomatoes,
waxy green peppers, a peach pressed firmly,
gently, from his palm to yours.
You can still feel the scars
from his roses. Your hand retreats.
Your fingers brush.
Your breath like a wave curls under, tumbles,
pulls back. Your belly tenses.
You are surfing, barely skimming the sand,
an unspeakable fear swelling your tongue.

Do not speak it.
This is what you were made for,
the heat of his gaze on your fore-arm,
burning your cheek.
You feel the slack first in your knees,
then your back. Do not succumb.
The best is still to come.

In the fall, he leaves in a glorious swirl
of gold and rust, amid the chatty travel songs

of migrating birds. You ache in his absence,
raking at the unreachable pain
in your chest. When you think of him,
you balk at his easy certainty,
his knowledge of your desire.
You delight in the melting snow-flakes
that catch in his hair.
You sigh at how his breathing undulates
under the white quilt. It is enough to lie
in bed on a slow Saturday,
to know he will come, his cool palm
stroking your belly, your breasts,
unexpectedly clutching your breath
as if it were another bouquet.

Do not hasten his wooing.
He will come soon enough.
You must not speak his name.
Only when you have slipped life's pearls
through your fingers, like a rosary,
counting the day after day
of his unfailing courtship,
when you have ached for him
in all the little things – in how you walk,
how your fingers probe a place for seeds,
how your cheek presses to his hard belly,
how you touch the mound where new life stirs –
only then will you be ready,
the light will break through
and the darkness, together,
and you will understand, finally,
who it is who has loved you
all this time, so well.

Beached

I focus on my breathing,
the full weight of all I have become
pressing gently, firmly down
against my ribs, the entering
and leaving of salt winds,
cries of sea birds
to my heart,
from all my heart.
The sun on my skin.

The sun on my skin
is dry-ness. Is death.
This body is made
for water.

I focus on the others
now, the young ones
slipping through the water,
water leaping ahead
of itself, its white ears flopping
ahead of itself, over the waves;
leaping into the air
they pass. The air is a challenge
for them, a thrill, a rush
of adrenalin. They
flute fountains. They fountain white
spitting hisses of joy.

If I make no sound
they will not see me.
If I cry
they will gather, they will mourn.
I will die seeing their sad eyes.
I want to die
full of ballet and bravado,
my mind a dance from water to air
to water, unthinking joy.

I make no sound, the wet
rock at my belly, the cool

water licking its slow
infinite sadness, the forgiveness of oceans,
the wisdom of heavy seas,
the sun at my back,
like a warm hand,
with each slowing breath
my spirits falling,

and rising.

A Pain with Nowhere to Run

This dusk, I am jogging between plots of fallow,
cassava and sugar cane, the Colombian night
creeping down from the mountains,
slipping & rustling among the cane leaves.
Birds startle and scold
the unexpected turbulence
of my passing.

After a day of arguing
complex systems and sustainable development,
attractors, gradients, and causal feedback loops,
I am running back
into my body.
I am searching for boundaries.
My hip aches. A few strides more
and deep pain seizes me.
I wonder if this is a boundary.
I keep thudding along, over the edge,
through a down-rush of endorphins,
then: nothing.

My thoughts have abandoned
me, trampled over each other,
burst in confusion from my hurly-burly brain
like terror-stricken dancers
fleeing a burning night club.
My God, what were we doing
in that place? they stumble
across furrows
into the slurred song of the swamp.

The frogs welcome my thoughts,
laughing like drunks in a bar.
Almost extinct, hemmed in by roads
and devious plots
of cane burning like hell
against the black velvet sky,

the frogs know
I can't be far behind.

Then, out of nowhere: whop!
The deep stab in the back.
This is where I discover no body no thoughts
and what remains:
that damned loopy heart of mine,
a pain with nowhere to run.
Whop! Whop! Whop!
like birds throwing their soft bodies against
the plate-glass of my living room
the memories are coming:
something stupid I said;
or just something stupid –
someone dead, or gone, or just over the cusp
slipping away into the basin
of another attractor;
my daughter, at three years,
toddling into my arms,
laughing;
my son playing
Chinese flute music
into the green summer dusk.
Letters not sent. Words unspoken.
Another bad joke
escaping my renegade mouth.
The perfect dinner – all the carrots
& green peppers, just so, sliced,
perfectly spiced and seared,
the guests gone home.
The scent of perfume
in an empty room. The touch of a hand.

The heart clenches with pain and joy.
This is the pain of the seventh orgasm,
the joy of giving my son a hug

after he piles all his things into the car,
my daughter before she goes through
airport security.

Still running, now,
because there's nothing else to do,
no help for it,
but to run into my body & through it,
clear out of my mind,
until all that's left
is this red, throbbing, glowing heart,
the only muscle really worth flexing,
the only one you can take with you,
looped and looping
out into the sibilant tropical night,
like a fat, star-crazy bird.

An Ordinary Life

In one alcove stands a young boy, delicate,
adored by little boy-cherubs
with perfectly parted hair.
Nearby, in the gloom of this
drab Cali cathedral, is another.
He is older. His mother was not so careful.
He fell among wine-bibbers,
gluttons and thieves. His head is gashed
with a crown of metal thorns, body mutilated,
contorted with pain.
This one is behind glass,
as if the priest fears more attacks.

The priest mutters
seductive chants into the half-light,
his half-listening flock
kneeling like scattered sheep
in the quiet forest of statues.

I shiver as I step from the church coolness
into the blinding sun.
In the city square, scarred old men
play board games;
a young man bends
over his typewriter,
an old woman across from him
speaking the words
his fingers clack onto the paper,
telling her loneliness to a child somewhere
in America.

I find myself worrying
about the prissy suburban boy-christ
and his california angels;
if he isn't careful,
he too may end up behind glass.
It can happen so fast.

How is it we are so easily seduced
by these plaster heroes?
We who cannot remember the holocaust
because we were not there,
we who are children of holocaust survivors
friends of those children,
children of holocaust perpetrators,
friends of those children,
ordinary jews muslims christians buddists agnostics
persons of a certain past
and an uncertain future,

we who suffer the ordinary,
something anyone can aspire to, who worry about
our children being out late,
jobs, hair, love – the prospect of losing them –
mortgages, car-rust,
the boy Jesus,

we whose suffering, we think, is so unlike
all that other suffering, the stuff that is beyond us:
clever tricks done with cigarettes, or electrical wires,
appropriate technology finely tuned,
children forced to shoot their friends,
those people, not like us,
hutus tutsis albanians kurds mayans
suffering for being born, for doing something,
or not doing something, for free trade, for faith,
for faithlessness, for drugs, for the war on drugs,

we whose unremarkable suffering
amounts to not having suffered,
knowing we are alone in the universe,
that this privileged loneliness
cannot last,

we must go on,
forever every day every moment
in the little things,
speaking hope speaking forgiveness
speaking broken-ness,
in a bus, next to the ordinary-looking man
in the straw hat, the man from behind the glass,
bumping in happy drunkenness, fearfully,
along the back streets of Cali,
singing.

II.
Grace Amid the Ruins

Going Home

In Nairobi, on the Kenyan high plateau,
the power stops.
The yard lights close their eyes.
The world disappears.
My computer screen hesitates,
goes into sleep mode.
I sit with a candle at a wooden table.
In the next room my friend John
reads to his daughters in the flickering light:
A Plague of Caterpillars.
Outside, cicadas mimic
high tension power lines.
They know they are winning.

In Kitchener, in the Canadian Great Lakes Basin,
crossing an asphalt plaza to the video store,
I am engulfed by a storm of anxious rocks
rushing past me, home to quarries;
car metals bleed into earth-wounds,
to veins deep in the rock bed.
Plastic from cars, packages of candy bars,
household cleaners, gasoline, oil – all those
slick talismans of modern life
dive through black pools,
emerge as prehistoric jungles.
Clothing leaps from store racks;
sheep graze in cotton fields.
Drunk on French wine, earthworms
step-dance & polka with farmers' sausage-
cum-rollicking pigs.
My leather shoes find their cows.
They are coming home,
like the chickens, to roost.

Somewhere between Nairobi and Kitchener,
naked, shivering in the dark,
I stand alone,

thinking about trees,
listening for cicadas,
silent now, magnanimous
in victory.

Outside my highland window,
a dog, hesitantly,
tries several wavering notes.

Teilhard de Chardin Surfs the Internet

We speak with voices
neither of men nor angels.
We speak with the ephemeral complexity
of electrons, a conversation
of sand castles, articulating perplexity,
retreating to a sigh of candy wrappers, pop cans,
foam and kelp-litter, scraps of garbage
information, dissimulation,
thoughts for gulls to squabble over.
And as the sea sucks back,
a crab, incredible, unthinking, hard
quotidian experience, a wonder of survival,
scuttles over the traces
of our castles. All over the world,
on the beaches of the internet,
you can hear the hissing intake of breath.
All of evolution's come to this
anticipation, this wondrous
rising wave. For just one cresting second,
in tightening bellies, tumbling over
flashing sand, stars, water, air,
and just before
the flotsam engulfs us,
we shall have spoken everything,
understood
nothing,
the sea will sigh,
and, rising sluggishly, heave:
just one more try.

What There Is

The leaf, unpuckered from its stem,
its slow waltz to the lawn,
winter's day into night;
a shoeless toddler, tumbling
like a die down the faecal-dewed cobbles
of Kathmandu, the dog-heaps, sighing,
the pre-dawn butchers' fires
along the sluggish river;
the man, unstuck in Montreal,
his heart, like a fox, pausing,
the unbearable beauty and sadness
of this damned forest, the sagging trunks and
quivering limbs, the barely restrained call
of Satchmo's eager hounds.
What cannot be done
will be imagined; the unimaginable
has long been managed. In Kitchener
a man mows the lawn. In Kathmandu
men with briefcases and backpacks rise
to the clouds, with a roar,
and disappear. In Montreal
two Maritimers, strangers adrift
at a sidewalk cafe, are signing;
their hands like fish leap, twist, dance
a ritual greeting amid the city's rip-tide surf.

Grace Amid the Ruins

All night
the dog on the roof next door barks.
At dawn, my body's temple echoes
with confused shouts and protests,
brain cells lie toppled,
tangled in ruin.
The hotel guard,
still half asleep
and wrapped in shawls,
releases through barred gates
this fool Canadian,
off for an early morning walk
through night-littered alleys.

Along the roof-line
of Kathmandu
silver satellite dishes are raised
like cupped hands
awaiting crumbs
from the gods:
news from Washington,
Frankfurt,
the Bombay movie scene.

In the asphalt street
a toddler squats
amid the litter of plastic bags,
green mango leaves, shattered red bricks,
squashed yellow-brown mottled bananas.
One of the storekeepers
from across the street
is throwing stones at her.
When she has made
her bile-ish pile,
she deftly drops her tattered hem
and scampers off.

A pre-teen girl
in an earth-tone plain and threadbare dress,
leans like a shaft of slim-limbed light
across a darkened doorway.
A boy, her age-mate, bold
in a clean white shirt
and pressed blue trousers,
self-consciously runs across her line of vision
to the neighbour's variety shop.
The wry light in her eyes
and the disdainful, one-sided uplift of her lips
tell all: no amount of red and white candy
offered from his hand
can save him.

A slender boy, all ribs and arms and legs,
shifting from foot to foot, shivers
in a bright blue tub, arms folded stoically.
His ten-year-old sister is splashing
water over his bony beige body,
rubbing him down with soap
and rags.
They burst out laughing
at the sight of me.

All day three ragged urchins
worked the crowds,
one rupee, one rupee,
their voices lingered over bright Gore-tex,
tugged at untucked, faded blue cotton.
Now, at dawn, like puppies,
they pile up at the roadside
in sighing sleep.

On the bridge over the Bishnumati
the vendors are laying out
their brass pots, cotton shirts, and fruit,

the tailors are tuning their machines.
Below, the pigs forage in offal
from slaughtered buffaloes
and open latrines.

The satellite dishes bring Bosnia,
Chechnya, Kashmir, Colombo,
the G-7 summit, *Seinfeld*, *Destiny Ridge*,
a new world economic order, *Mad About You*,
beheaded tourists, *Friends*,
Shwartzenegger, Schwartzkopf.
Men in dark suits
pose for the camera. A voice says
they are making progress.

I look to the hills,
the mountains cloaked in grey rain.
From whence will come our help?
From whence the world's end?
The courage to endure?

The girl on the sidewalk
very carefully stacks her lychees and peaches
in pyramids of five.
With nimble grace and dignity
she crosses her legs
and waits.

A Cold Night in Kathmandu

I.

Because I came in on a jet
and was served champagne
Because they slaughter buffaloes wash clothes squat
drink water along the banks of the Bishnumati
Because they eat rice twice a day
with a bit of sauce
Because I had a hot shower
Because I use toilet paper
Because a group at the table next to mine
in the restaurant where I am overfilling on Thai food
is planning the ultimate descent
pristine whitewater rafting
in the flush of youth European
Aussie American Canadian youth that is
the big thrill of riding the natural power
of rice paddy soil farmers' livelihoods
bridges to market washed out down in the brown torrent
flooding the plains fantastic! Let's go down again!
Because of course they don't think of it that way,
exactly,
Because an environmental T-shirt is an insult in Kathmandu
like a holocaust T-shirt in Jerusalem,
beyond tacky, a quiet humiliation
Because in the cold dry mountainous air
the shit of trekkers is forever preserved
Because I too love the thrill of fresh air water
mountain views the rush of adrenalin,
I took off my "Veterinarians for the Environment"
                    T-shirt in Kathmandu.

II.

I put my "Veterinarians for the Environment" T-shirt back on
                    in Kathmandu
because I got cold at night.

The Wisdom of the East

In frayed jeans and loosely fitting faded-saffron shirts, two gaunt and unsexed, lanky foreigners rush forward beaming and bowing, to greet the old Buddhist monk emerging from Tribhuvan Airport in Kathmandu. He obliges them by draping a white shawl over each of their shoulders. They follow respectfully, faces masked with beatific smiles. He pushes ahead with his baggage cart. Along with the usual maroon gown of the Buddhist monks, he is wearing a fedora and shiny leather platform boots. His cart stacked high with new suitcases, he smiles, absently, in the manner of a pleased grandfather or a satisfied storekeeper.

The Fat Lady Struck Dumb
It ain't over till the fat lady sings

A soft swarm of lost voices, like rare, muffled pink
pigeons, rumples the smooth summer air:
sighs of Spanish, chortled slav-tongues, warbled
Englishes of England, Jamaica, India,
the grackled Frenches of Quebec, Haiti, Algeria, Paris,
Hindis of Vancouver, London, Delhi,
Arabics of Sudan, Somalia, Jordan;
the trees tremble with the flap and squabble
of a thousand sausages with sauerkraut,
empanadas flocking and swooping,
and fluttering scents
of salsa, cinnamon and baklava.

In Victoria Park, City of Kitchener,
Canada Day, beneath the statue of Queen Victoria,
the Empire of the Dispossessed
strikes back.

Still, I stand amid chill
airstreams they have surfed to come here,
ragged winds filling sails of union jacks
fleur de lis stars stripes crosses crescents,
the snarling
downdrafts of nationhood.
They have come for dancing, justice,
fresh pastry, a kiss on the cheek,
a decent job, no guns at the grocery store.
They have come to circle the statue of the fat lady,
to drape her with a lacy shawl of droppings.
They have come to nest
nibble scratch poke together a new place,
a new country, another world.

The prickly grass of home puckers at our bare soles,
welcomes us with a big open-mouthed kiss,
loving us, devouring us,
bringing us into the old Canadian family.

Singing above, we are joined
from below by our country's founders, a vast, Wagnerian
harmony tongue-tickling our arches,
la-di-da-ing at our backs, tum-tiddling our bones,
humming in the stem cells at the marrow's heart,
twisting in the ancient codes
that make us
who we are: the Auruch, the Quagga,
Gypsonia, Dickinsonia, Glyptodont,
the Moa, the Ammonites, the Trilobites,
the chorus bursting through us, from us,
poetry of the Burgess Shale and the Skeleton Coast,
trios of Leaky's Lucy, Java Man,
and my grandmother:
here we come, the Canadian Val-kyrie eleisons
singing as we tumble,
tongue to tongue,
a giant wave roaring and hissing head over heels
across time's shifting strand.

Before us, mouth gaping, swept up, uprooted
in our uproarious tide,
the fat lady, once puffed up with
gall and bold pronouncements
on her pedestal, now helpless as the flightless kakapo,
is struck
dumb.

The Olympic Thinking Competition

The best ideas begin in the small
of your back and ascend,
vertebra by vertebra, slowly,
methodically. You can't quite tell
what they are, or what they are feeling.
You can feel their toes gripping
the rungs. They are slightly
wet. They are young and muscular.
This may take days, or months, or years.
Occasionally, a decade
or more. A slight quiver
descends your spine
as they near the top. You can feel
the fingers, strong and wrinkled
from long hours of swimming,
pull back slightly. Then the feet
overtake the hands, the palms
push down against the top of your head
and lift free.
Now you can feel her full weight.

She moves forward across your brain.
No matter how hard you try
to look upward,
you cannot see her.
Briefly, she pushes down on your
cerebrum, and, for a second,
you think this has all been
for nothing. Your head feels empty.
You want to cry out your frustration and fear,
your anger at being so, so human.

Arms wide as wings,
she soars past you, firmly, perfectly
in tune with herself.
You think she might be smiling,
just slightly. Droplets of water and sun commingled
run like soft jewels down her legs, belly, breasts,

the slim line of her head, hair tucked up
under a snug cap.
In a flash you feel pure passion, inspiration, love.
There is a milli-second of lust,
as you think you might, for once,
possess such beauty,
such perfect coordination.

The best ideas somersault
three times, stretch and point
like rare marine cats,
and disappear into the aquamarine
noosphere.

You sit by the pool-side,
remembering, trying to re-create the scene
for others. It was like...you see...
It was...
You try essays, poems,
story-telling, mathematical formulae,
scientific papers.

After all your other thoughts
have gone home,
you doze by the darkened pool-side,
turning a glass of red wine in your hand.
Ripples from her passing
spread gently across your thoughts.

The Squirrels

To Faris, from Jordan,
the elephants at the Toronto zoo
are of no interest. He wanders
around our back yard photographing squirrels.

They are everywhere – a profusion of jittery wild things,
chasing each other around and around
the tree trunks, leaping, surprise!
from the compost hole,
when the lid is lifted,
teasing the cat with jiggling tails
and chatter-calls,
scrabbling in the insulation above our bedroom,
gathering on the peak of the roof at first light
to survey the park across the road.

Faris is not there as I listen
to the Radio Noon call-in show.
The exterminator gives advice
about bush rats. It takes me a moment
to realize that this is his name
for squirrels. They can cause
a lot of damage to your summer
cottage, but some excellent poisons
are now available.

I sit at a picnic table
eating my lunch. At the far end,
a squirrel sits, still as a pine cone,
the perfect camouflage from hawks and owls.
He wonders if it will work on me.
Faris, me, the exterminator
all look the same to him.
His tail is curled up along his back
like a question mark.

Recognition

We eye each other,
the raccoon and I, he with my garbage,
me with my sense of order disturbed.
He is re-ordering my garbage.

He is calculating the value
of chicken bones, my threat-potential,
the distance to the nearest
tree. I am calculating
the genetic distance between us.

When I climb into my car
by the curbside, he watches
from the branch
just above my head.

I do not know, nor does he,
the meaning of this encounter.
Driving away,
I ponder how selfish genes
can produce self-reflective
thoughts with delusions
of rationality.

The raccoon is carefully
arranging his dinner.

The Better Part of the Day
Sauble Beach, Lake Huron

The day comes shuffling in slow
waves along the sand,
sibilant, obsequious.
His eyes avoid the radiant face,
his tousled and bejewelled queen.
He knows what she wants: romance
pencilled on an envelope,
her golden hair
across his pillow.

Staring at time's turned-back sheets,
where lake meets sky, his mind becomes
a window without curtains,
a room without furniture.

Gulls drift past
like children's voices,
strewing shrill hosannas.
The teasing queen slinks down
to meet his line of vision.
She turns, and diamonds shower
down the nimbo-cirrus
tumble of her hair.

The day grasps within himself;
tearing out his heart,
he holds it high, this gift,
this tiny, trembling rodent;
the scent of salt marsh
and lost poems pass
whispering
through his emptiness.

He turns now from his bright desire.
Muscle throbbing in cupped palms,
he walks into the rustling,
green-brown darkness.

Scrawny corn stalks,
rotting from the cold and rain,
squelch underfoot.

In the room in his head
a farmer scribbles sad sums
at a scratched wooden table.

The day sets down his heart
at the door to this room.

He knows his queen.
He knows she will return
for this. Smiling, he can already see
the farmer, staring through
cracked panes at the bedazzling
sunrise, plotting how
to salvage his corn.

Silver Bird on High

The sky is clear blue,
except for fluffs of pink cloud
like dust bunnies along the ruffled horizon
where the sun reclines.

A sleek, winged silver body
inscribes an unequivocal, simple,
mathematically pure line
across the sky's empty page.

Unlike the creatures
in the dark foliage nearby,
this bird neither flutters nor swoops,
neither dives nor flaps nor darts,
does not pause to poke a long nose
into a flower, nor dance,
tip to tip, in twilight.

It moves calmly, controlled,
like a banker among farmers,
like the Titanic
among chunks of water.

Down on the sidewalk
a congregation of pine cones
spills out into the street,
amid a jabbering choir of grackles,
singing exuberant, out-of-control
gospel. I walk among them
barely restraining the urge
to kick up my heels.
Two people, sitting
on a front porch
sipping drinks,
observe as I walk past.

The big silver bird
is sliding smoothly down toward
the Toronto airport.

There, dazed occupants
will hug their welcomers.
For a second, caught equivocally
between the airplane's perfection
and a lifetime of ordered aspirations,
they will forget who they are
supposed to be, forget,
just for a reckless moment,
their dignity, just
let go and squeeze,
whirl in unthinking joy.

They will step outside,
a suitcase in each hand.
One of them will look up:
a sheer scarf of birds
waving across the full round
face of the moon.

Love and Chaos

When a man and a woman
love each other
they are like two confused
caterpillars, their firm limber bellies
stuffed to exhaustion with green
leafy succulence, wound around each
other in impossible knots, a tangle
of wriggling footsies, hair caught
on their tongues, weaving
about themselves
a single luminous
cocoon
from which, as from
another womb, they slip & rise
on warm uplifts
on wings knit from the inner glow
of pale-fleshed deep cave animals, brushing across
the morning a brilliant storm
of colours, fields of daffodils
daisies iris flame trees draped
with bougainvillea & aurora borealis.

The chaos of their quivering celebration
creates hurricanes a world away
down golden streets; in banks
and office towers the men in power
tremble against their panes
to see the dervish fire, the black
laughing cloud like a prairie storm front
in a roaring whimpering
happy howl shattering
glasses in the mini-bar;
they brace themselves, one hand on the vault,
one hand in your pocket,
in a sudden silence dreaming
of white marble, of Sistine chapels,
deep memories of sunlight

through stained glass,
stunned, weeping on their backs
in three-piece suits,
a blizzard of burst feather pillows
leaf storms empty cocoons, a fount
of squandered larval possibilities
washing over them.

And driving blindly home at dusk
the smoky oil-on-canvas shades – redyellowpeach
aquamarine – are all but palpable,
as if from this one love we almost
see through veils of time's
pollution, the masterpiece
behind, the painting we could be,
once were, still are deep
deep inside,
returning to that single point
pre space pre time
laying our cheeks on pillows
of butterfly wings;
drifting to sleep our eyelids flutter
like love, falling in;
we murmur of rising heat,
of unclaimed aching limbs, of fevered skin,
of Michelangelo & Rubens & Rafael,
of fire and flight,
of wet & slightly salty, rumpled
sheets, while outside
down the dawn-grey streets drift
shreds of poetry.

John Donne Meets Chaos Theory

Ah love, please turn me not away,
for by the wings of butterflies
come hurricanes, and by the flutter of our eyes
the universe is changed.
This one small move,
our hands, our bodies rising,
falling, alters affairs from sheets to skies
until the earth our love becomes.

If this seems unconvincing, dear,
then think of us as dust caught
on a cosmic point, our wandering hands,
loose tongues & tousled hair
no consequence. So, all or naught,
which stirs your breast to rise or knees to bend?

Grace in Mid-Winter

Winter is an orphaned coast
abandoned by its sea, a mockery
of salt and sand along the walk
to keep me on the path, secure.
No sea birds, but the bleak wind's howl,
no hopes for safe return
of sailors, no ecstasy, no fear.

I came upon a small green place,
a tree with leaves in conversation, a Boomslang, or a vine.
I held a peach against my cheek. You nursed my pain.
I paused, and, for a second, felt at peace.

Winter is an argument
I cannot win. Down the deserted street
I rage. I name the season
all those words that have no home.
No wisdom here, just boredom's
endless lists, no wit but snow's
all censoring, white-out reign.

The Amateur

The woman in front of me
at the bank machine
turns sideways and disappears.
"Must be one of those ballerinas or gymnasts,"
I remark to the man behind me,
"a real pro."
He is staring at where I should be
and I realize: he can't see me
from this angle. I pirouette
and guffaw. Seeing me now, he knows
I am an amateur,
and intently checks his pocket organizer
for missed appointments.

In this city of homo economicus,
abstracticus, bottom-line-icus,
everywhere, on the bus,
at the office, canadicus, francoamericanus,
anti or pro, this is the crime:
that a man can still be amateur,
uncertain, seen, obscenely, from all angles,
practising at his humanity, asking
what it means, that he can offer flowers,
make faces at the baby in the grocery cart,
dig into his pockets for change at the cashier,
have to put back the cookies,
that he might try his hand
at baking a pie with fresh-sliced apples,
bloody his finger at the counter,
at the end of a long day at the office
make a mess of supper,
raise a glass of wine,
say something utterly inappropriate,
crudely sexual, religious, political,
some gut feeling surfacing,
the soul's loch monster gasping for air,
or speak of rainy evenings
and empty streets at dawn,
or, without irony, lament his success,

or cry in the bathroom,
for no reason he can think of,
or laugh at Saturday cartoons.

And everywhere, standing in line at the grocery store,
looking up from a pile of papers
in some professor's office,
or drunk, begging a loonie for coffee in front of the bank,
there are people in this city
without poems, their own poems,
in this city where books are balanced,
not read or celebrated,
when everywhere the words are trashed,
tongue-lashed, and trod upon,
when so little is required
to fashion a few lines, to weave a garland
from the litter
of our daily speech, a gift for having lived
another day amid the fragile, happy
babble of a family, the info-streets strewn
with the pulp and wreckage of our public cant,

so little to dream on, to suckle hope's gaunt baby.

Take these lines. Take these lines,
these unpeeled syllables left lying
on the table, next to an empty glass,
next to a flag, just another coloured napkin,
red and white blue and white, whatever,
in the silence, right there
at the Interac, at the checkout,
cup them in your hands,
hum a tune for no reason,
turn yourself around and around and
all around you, homo categoricus,
pigeon holicus, will stare at you
suddenly, brashly, blushingly visible.

You can feel them in your palm
like tiny squabs
scrabbling for crumbs.

I Cannot Love You, Without

Without touching my fingers to the earth
you walk on, without tonguing like a cow
the grass, the leaves after the light crush
of your passing, rising again
with slow dignity, without nosing
the ants strung out in their complex symphony
of songlines, without loving the long pause
of the earthworms as they feel the sweet
cocky song of a robin, the long pause of the cat
as she views the robin's bob,
I cannot love you.

Raising to you the ruby's crystal blush
of red Chilean wine, I raise a glass
to the men and women whose coarse palms plucked
this harvest, to the children with no shoes.
I cannot love you without remembering
how they poke around the barrios
overturning rocks, reading the pattern
of bugs there for some sign of a future,
how they sell cigarettes and oranges
to motorists at stoplights.
I cannot touch you without embracing
all those splintered children
axed by the insatiable neatness of book-keepers,
kindling for a fearful sacrifice
to science and lust,
gently gathering them
into my arms. I cannot hold them
without remembering you, without losing myself
in our daily conversation, the mingling
of our voices, which goes nowhere,
and is everything.

I break this bread with you.
We dip it into swirls of cheese.
We share a trust with dust-browed farmers,
robbed at pen-point, caught in the cross-fire
of demands for Kodak-perfect cornucopias,

and un-farmed wilderness.
With weary coffee pickers and sugar cutters
we dance, in muffled happiness,
the arm-locked, slow-kicking yarn of us weaving
among the glittering sparks of feral cats,
homeless wolves, whiskered rats,
sighing waves of murmuring birds.
I love them with my heart pounding,
laughing out loud. With a rush
of understanding I want to flee, stumbling, away.
I want to charge into the teeth and claws of them,
into their wild, devouring lust for us.

I cannot love you without being made small,
a fearful, feathered, fallen parakeet,
un-nested on the forest floor.
And in the throes of my
o-pinioned love, you will feel the scratch
of my toenails climbing
your sighs and flowers, returning
from the earth, from all the brown
leaf-wilting weariness of it,
with aching muscles returning
to the heights of you,
to the green trembling canopy,
where, in the blue, bright sky above,
in a sudden, furious
squall of petals,

we shall fall again, softly, like a gentle rain
through the long resplendent evening.
Into the furrow of our brows,
into the arms of all we have remembered
into the comforter of all their million voices
whispering, beyond the pain of all remembrance,
our mud-caked bodies shall unfurl,
our hair a tangled nest for seeds,
fallen leaves, and lost children.

We shall awaken in the green half-light.

Concatenations

Until that loving leap in the Hoosier dark,
I paid no mind to cats.

At five years old, I had wandered
away from home
down a long treed Winnipeg street
in search of ice-cream.
The neighbour's cat came partway
up the block, then abandoned me
for birds. The cat was out of the bag.
I knew then I would forever,
like a cat, be alone.

At nineteen,
I wandered around the world.
I do not remember cats
in London, Heidelberg,
Istanbul, Kathmandu,
Delhi, Bangkok ... all those other
cities that were not Winnipeg.
I had not read T.S. Eliot on cats,
and would not have predicted
a stage musical. Girls, in those days,
still made catty remarks and
had pussies, real men made catcalls,
and were not afraid of catwalks
high above the city.
It was a dog's life,
for a boy afraid of heights,
an un-cool cat
barely out of Mennonite catechism,
lost in those erotic catacombs.

Then, the irreversible catapult
in the Hoosier dark, the long-clawed kitten,
Raspberry, clinging gleefully
to my backside
in the storm-tossed sea
of our too-thin sheets. I was not sorry

to leave him behind as we headed north.
In Saskatoon, Mozart, the regal, silver long-hair,
once, still kittenish, almost drowned attempting to drink
from the toilet bowl, had us evicted
when, frustrated and wet,
standing next to me, fresh from the shower,
he confronted the old landlady
as she nosed her uninvited way
into our no-pets apartment.
Later, he welcomed our first child,
passed him the job of educating us,
and vanished into the prairie snow.

We replaced him, out of pity,
with a congenitally retarded male.
Resisting the biological determinism of veterinary science,
he denounced his castration by
spraying doors and carpets.
In this, he merely reflected the chaos
of a life with two diaper-bottomed children in Grand Prairie,
Alberta. He was last reported rehabilitating
among succulent mice, warm hay-beds,
open latrines and the unconditional charity
of young Hutterite girls.
Many young parents
have fantasies of doing the same,
though most make do
with brief, recuperative cat-naps in the TV room.

Puff the First, smuggled into married student housing,
later registered under a temporary amnesty,
died with a mouse in her teeth, crossing a highway
in Guelph, Ontario – a happy death,
despite my caterwauling heart.

Puff the Second, selected from a farm to be
Puff the First resurrected, so as to match
the description on the amnesty registration papers,
fiercely loyal, demanding the same,

urinated on my side of the bed
when we went on a brief vacation,
grew to lionesque proportions,
learned, finally, the patience
that comes with inner power,
a good, quick set of teeth and claws,
and a two year legal separation
while we escaped to Indonesia.

Puff the Third, the slim Javanese rice-eater,
was our C-section queen, tied on her back
on the cold steel table, anaesthetized
from the waist down, astounded from the head up,
her self-image forever changed,
a crowd of eager veterinary students
peering into the mysteries of her abdomen.

On our return, Puff the Second's territory encompassed
a whole city block, in which
all other cats rolled over and paid homage,
and wandering, witless strangers
paid their dues in tufts of fur.
But even kings can suffer
urinary blockage;
he disappeared a thousand dollars later,
his penis removed
and his genitalia rebuilt.
And now forever re-appears
on strange street corners
and in dreams, bearing essential,
ambiguous messages.

Tigger, the Ontario farm fighter, who leapt out at anyone
anytime, anywhere and finally attacked one car too many,
was buried illegally, covered with tulips, appropriately,
fierce romantic that he was,
by the lilac bushes.

And now, le Gateau, Kathleen's birthday cake,
the one I come home to,
grow old with, the patient, graceful queen,
no territorial demands
beyond the picnic table on the deck, or slightly more,
perhaps the back yard, when we accompany her,
rolls onto her back to exercise with me
in the morning, on the kitchen floor,
provided I brush her with one hand,
while doing pelvic tilts.
She purrs calmly in my lap, listening to my worry
over the power of book-keepers
and right wing politicians, then quick and cat-like
sinks her teeth into my hand
for no apparent reason, a sudden, inexplicable desire,

a reminder: we're still here
aren't we? They haven't got us yet,

the dogs.

Where the Day Goes

The cat is like a day
that waits for you
dreaming of something mice
on the doily by the window

while you are
squirreling nuts away
busily busily all day working
until, opening the kitchen door
you pause, listen for the claws'
prickle prickle
over the hardwood.

Too late
you see her
thinking:
the mouse is home.

You, bits of fluff and weary bone,
slouch
on the couch,

another bewhiskered day
purring in your lap,
pawing her nose.

The Sanitary Dream Engineers

This is the stuff of dreams –
the leftovers from your day,
all the things you couldn't fit in
anywhere: the really bad TV show,
pictures of a government minister
handing the keys of your house
to the bank manager,
your fear of being lost with a full bladder
in a bathroom-less labyrinthine building,
soldiers storming a bus full of hostages,
a cryptic message from the President,
the meeting you missed with your Department Chair,
that egomaniacal academic colleague
you criticized, the shoot-out at the post office,
someone murdered, perhaps by you,
while you were talking to Princess Di
on a cell phone,
the student whose dress you accidentally
saw down, those squirrely feelings
you'd buried, like nuts and diamonds,
suddenly unearthed, in mud and melting snow,
and a bright blue sky,
the crow banging his reflection
at your office window, day in day out,
so perfectly adapted to your daily routine,

all those things
that should have been in your poetry,
the things that are so clear
at two in the morning, just
as they are being trucked away.
You see the guy in coveralls
dumping several perfect poems
into the fine paper bin.
You are too sleepy to stop him.
You lie awake the rest of the night,
with your legs crossed,

trying to remember your dreams.
You think of a garbage truck
disappearing down an empty street.

Sometimes you toss the name
of someone essential to your happiness,
written on the back of a grocery list,
into the recycling box.
The engineers do not sort for you;
they take everything.
When you meet that person the next day
you will not know them.
Sometimes it is the name of a deadly virus,
the number of cases of foodborne illness in Canada,
an important message from the person
whose name you can't remember,
or the weight of a hand touching you
in kindness, or abuse;
sometimes it is a couple of lines,
a turn of phrase, that inadvertently
ends up in the trash, or an idea
that might have saved the world your family
your marriage, or a lint-covered
lump of sugar you could have given someone
in passing, or something bitter
to ponder in the routine sweetness
of a day, something to clear
the mental palate.

As you get older, more and more gets thrown out,
all the recent stuff.
The drawers and closets and cubbyholes are full of
1066 and All That,
the number and street of the house you lived in
when you were five and ran away from home,
Wendy, whose pony tail you dipped
into the inkwell in Grade Five,
what you *should* have said
to the school bully,

the walking dandruff rabbit mite, *Cheyletiella*,
the sheep fluke *Dicrocoelium dendriticum*,
the easy way to castrate a bull.
These are the things that will still
be with you when you are ninety.
That publisher you met yesterday
who promised you a big advance?
His name is already hauled away.

Oh my friends who aspire
to write poetry, this is your aspiration –
to be a cell phone,
a soldier, a dress, a bladder,
a lonely urinal no one can find,
a case of food poisoning, a banker.
Each morning
you will turn the empty coffee mug
in your hands, searching
for meaning in the dregs.
You will stick your nose into it.

This is the desire that wracked
your spirit, the vision
you were offered,
unasked for,
what is no longer there,
what you have lost.

Tonight, the sanitary dream engineers
will take even that away.
Tomorrow, you will have to begin again
at the bottom
of another cup of coffee.

III.

Coyotes

Temple at Dusk

Mist settles like a shawl
over the bent old mountains,
white water unravelling
over gnarled ribs of fallen trees
and belly-smooth stones.
Somewhere near, whispered the old woman,
there is a temple.
Stepping from one stone to the next, I slip.
Ice bites my thigh.
Closing in from the lean trees
along the shore,
dark robes fold and billow.
Through the fog,
a bell's clear song.

World Peace: December, 1968, Hokkaido

In December, the farmers
on Hokkaido
sit around the woodstove
telling stories. Grinning,
they pour me another glass of saké
and tell me I shall bring peace to the world.
I have hitch-hiked here
to visit Kazuo,
fellow-vagabond on the boat
from Bangkok.
The farmers are Kazuo's uncles.

They bring out his cousin
to entertain me.
I am twenty years old.
She is seventeen.
I think she is beautiful.
At least, that being the limit
of my Japanese,
is what I tell her.
That, and *I love you.*
At this point, I believe
I *will* bring peace to the world,
that this stirring of my senses *is* love.

We sit in silence after
everyone has gone
to bed, the embers not yet died.
She pours me tea.

Later, I lie
under a warm quilt
my spirit like breath
hovering near the frosty ceiling,
thinking about farmers,
Japanese girls,
world peace, my bladder,
and where down that cold dark hallway
she might be sleeping.

Mountains: a Poem for the Millennium

In a radiant cloud
at the top of the ski lift
I turn and wrestle
my grandmother and her siblings
off my back;
they cling to me. I pry away their fingers.
They scream after me in the cold white fog.
They thought I would stay with them,
that I'd bring them back down
with me. It is my duty
to leave them here.

There is a whole crowd of them
up here: Québecois, Blacks,
Native Americans, Cambodians, Jews, Women,
Mennonites, Timorese, Tibetans, Doukhobours,
Communists, Democrats,
those who were tortured,
anguished once-torturers,
those who wished they had been either
one or the other, claiming a crown
of righteousness or infamy,
all my relatives,
the whole hurting congregation of the 20th century.

I fall away from them into the hissing mist,
this mantra thrumming after me:
Never forget!

It is one thing to remember,
another for me to carry them –
my father, my aunt Mary,
in-laws, second great uncles
once removed – clinging to my neck until
down at the club-house,
the church, the town hall,
I dump them before the crowd, glaring,

okay, see what you did?
Now how will you give us justice?
This would be the worst abuse of all –
to use my forbears
as a moral shield.
Je me souviens: the wail
of their outraged voices whips icily after me
down the mountain.

My son and daughter ski ahead,
leaping a dance of red and navy blue,
into the clouds.
They are my guides
over the waves of ice, between
stark, congregated, trees,
rock altars,
the reckless zen of snow-boarders
appearing disappearing.
Je me souviens
my death, my obligations.

Behind me, at the top,
it's closing time, lights out.
The world that was, was hoped for,
shall not be. We let the past lead
at our peril; retrospective justice
is revenge, a ski jump to the rocks.
Our hope is this: to let our children
deftly lead among the pines
where justice kindles, waiting.

I remember hiking down
from cool Himalayan views,
a light pack on my back,
to blistering heat, hobbling lost
near a medieval city,
red stone raised up
against the shimmering green.
I remember the boy

who led me, this fool Canadian,
through the slippery muck
of rice fields, across the river
up another slope.

I recall the ancient temple,
old men's faces in the grey wood,
calling forth in silence the silence deep
in me, and the kid, having charmed me out of
all my pencils, a peach, some granola bars,
a handful of rupees,
with a quick smile, quick wave, gone.

I cannot say I doubted him.

I strain my eyes
into the darkening mist,
a blind man seeing only shapes now.
Skimming breakneck
over moguls between trees
I call after them,
a chill in my trachea,
as they disappear,
my breath snagged, doubting

the slope below, sighing at the snow spray
of our stop. Tomorrow
they will bear me up
and set me down
up there, complaining, with my ancestors,
by heaven's chilling gate.

But for this evening,
stinging toes next to the stone-bound fire,
hot chili, toast, a few songs will suffice,
while, just once more,
I share my tale,
and a long slow sipping
of hot cider with stick cinnamon.

Big White, Canada and Nagarkot, Nepal.

The Three Stations of Montreal

You begin on your knees,
dragging yourself, joint by aching joint,
up the stairs at St. Joseph's Oratory
to the great grey patriarchal dome.
At the top, you see a flickering
old movie about Brother André's dedication
to building this place, and why
you should be grateful. You see
his heart in a jar. The weight
of this Stalinesque monument
is enough to make many people
throw away their crutches.

After you have dumped
your suffering, you visit
Notre Dame Basilica,
where everything is light and dark commingled,
men, women, children, Europeans,
Indians, the cross in the chapel rising
ambiguously from a tangled garden
of lost humanity. Dust motes dance
and jump on Mozartian light streams
tumbling down from stained glass
windows through the knavish air.
When you step outside,
you are humming.
You take someone's hand,
go for a glass of wine
and some chocolate.
You realize that you understand
nothing, that life is redolent
with grace
and pointlessness.

And now your journey takes you
past a neighbourhood of roses
a choir of half-unbuttoned,
red-pink and salmon-petalled

Renoiresque maidens,
leaning this way and that,
puffing and giggling in the summery gusts,
in their green finery,
trying to catch your attention,
so ebulliently beautiful you must
avert your eyes, fearing
a twinge of lust,
your daughter
might be among them,
your wife
might notice you staring.
You might grasp at some memory
from your youth – another sucker
for the California quest market.
This is not your destination.

This is the Montreal Botanical Gardens.
This is the path to the Orient.
Beyond the blush of roses:
carefully selected stones
from China and Quebec,
gnarled trees, shrubs, lilies, small arched bridges,
bonsai-shrines, gravel raked like sulci in the brain,
and water paths for slow, fat, golden fish.
Step around a rock-crag corner:
there is a pond, a tree, a vista
from China to Japan, from the sky into the pit
of your confusion.

Speechless, you stand as the rain-squall
wraps its arms around your body,
and draws you to itself. There are rainbows
and scudding black clouds
across the clean, rain-washed blue,
and the whiff of earth, rotting leaves,
wilting wet flower petals
and small green shoots.

Bringing Home the Groceries

Behind a woman at the check-out counter
the unexpected thought, in full living colour,
hits you in the diaphragm:
you want to be inside her.

You imagine yourself in a gelatin capsule,
Dristan, say, or a vitamin,
slipping past the tongue;
you feel the soft slime of it
as you close your eyes for the sudden drop
down the fleshy chute, with a scream and a splash
plunging through a whirlpool of stomach acid.
You hope you didn't actually say something
out loud. You are checking
your pocket for the right change.
You see yourself beached among the villi,
bile and enzymes licking at your toes.
What is all this stuff?
I didn't ask for this, you say.

You would not believe all the wild places
there are in an ordinary person
buying chips and Drano at the express checkout
(eight items or less).
You would not believe the baked rocks
against your feet, the sun clinging
to your back as you clamber inland
through portal veins,
past the Islets of Langerhans,
flung topsy-turvey against all odds
with a manic boom
through the blood-brain barrier.
How could you describe the bright dash
of wildflowers amid the prickly shrubs?
How could you explain the ache
of too little time, too many items
too little cash, your heart uprooted,
littering the mud and stone

with bits of muscle, veined leaves,
fragments of capillaries,
a grab-bin of alternate lives
reduced for quick sale?
No one would believe you.
That person was a housewife, they would say,
so-and-so's sister, a milk-and-cookies girl
with well-trod paths
well-known to all. No one would believe
you had sailed the offal current
to such a strange, sun-bitten place.

And if you'd gone there,
why would you come back?
Getting into your car
with a block of lard and eight firm apples,
surveying the banal madness of the parking lot,
you imagine yourself with Drano and Ruffles
surveying the same banality,

and imagine you could have stayed there,
had another life, another time,
but you know you would already be missing
where you are, where you are going,
to become a root memory in your family tree,
the clink of forks on stoneware
as the kids scrape up
another of your perfect apple pies,
with their teenage impatience to be somewhere else,
with someone else,
not knowing that a flaky crust and watery fruit
is not dessert, is you,
now permanently inside them,
forever coming home.

Birthday Anti-Poem

The length of Ireland's coastline, says Mandelbrot,
is dependent on the units of measure –
the smaller the units, the longer the coastline.
Eventually, at the infinite limit of minutiae,
the coastline of Canada
and the coastline of Ireland
and the coastline of your heart
are equal.
This is chaos theory.

Sing this antiphonally.
Sing this as an antipasto
for birthdays:

the length of your life
depends on how often you celebrate
time's passage.

The world is full of slippery, newborn Methuselahs,
celebrating breath by gurgling breath,
teenaged Saras out for a weekly good time,
and middle-aged Lot's wives
looking back at life,
struck, suddenly, by their age.

By the time we are measuring decades,
we weary of all this.
We invent new theories of time.
This is just chaos.

Sing, rather, the antiphrasis of the oyster,
who, asked his age,
opens his mouth: a pearl.
You are speechless, and in that flash,
everything has been said.

Only when we become old as children,
at the limit of our ability
to process birthday poems,

losing count,
when all the candles waver in a blur,
will we return to ourselves,
our unfathomable thoughts
slippery with meconium.

In that moment when,
from the perfect grace of being in time,
we have learned to sing unceasingly,
the echoes resonating back
from the antipodes of every moment,

the birthday poem will disappear.
There will be a cat
breathing the rhythms of mystery
in your lap.

For Mother: Weinachtswuensch 1995

From splintered books
and un-leafed trees of knowledge
we clamber over branches
of distracting thought, back
down the long haul,
soul-deep in clinging muck
to this un-bowed
still-warm place:
the little kitchen that you've built,
refuge of rye and gingerbread,
röllche, peppermint cookies,
and your deep and wrinkled grace.

Listen: you've heard all this before –
the encircling whirlwind of self-righteous
wrongers of all rights
tearing down the walls,
unroofing shelters, promising
a better home, a bright new day,
and freedom's flight, delivering
shiny wallpaper, thatch, birdless bills
and this cursed, cold, unruly night.

But now, here in the centre
of the whistling dark,
warmed at your embers' long, deep glow,
it is enough to pause
and wonder, and, knowing you,
to know possibilities, that we may someday too
from all that glorious wreckage
select a moment here,
a splash of water, a shard of sun,
a hand's touch, a sugar-bun,
rough board and hand-sewn curtain,
a passing comment there,
constructing for *our* children
just such a table, just such chairs,

where we can sit, in respite
from time's ceaseless wear,

where wisdom, joy and private grief
whisper their rich, uncommon scents

of the consoling rye-bread's dark
and rising loaf.

Flower Gardening

Rebecca calls from Germany.
She is studying in a breathless frenzy –
dreams in German French doing well
in school, dancing the nights away
waltzes fox trots they have champagne
sambas rumbas might not be home
for Christmas studying Jesus in religion class
how are we anyway?
She sees her reflection on the window.
imagines herself
by another window, her thoughts
unravelling down the empty snow-bound street
at dusk. The only cure, she thinks, is more
dancing.

Kathy is in the garden
cutting back the ferns and lilies,
leaving a trail of crumbly brown-leafed skirts
and upturned soil; free of roots
and obligations, it sighs
in the apple-crisp fall air,
empty, satisfied.

She kneels now
by the roses, lost in thought,
crumbling cakes of soil into her palm.
From a riffling shawl
of green and leafy fans
draped down the darkening fence behind her,
peeks a chorus of coy blue
morning glories.

Matthew
for high school graduation

Once, toddling in the tousled earth
and shrubs behind our townhouse at the edge
of Bear Creek, Alberta, re-named Grande Prairie
by the Chamber of Commerce,
me the young father-veterinarian keeping
half an eagle eye on your little creatureliness,
knowing what names cannot hide,
that shadows with warm, humid breath
still ambled through the bush,
pawing behind trees for honey, grubs and little boys,
you tumbled back toward me with only one shoe
and I knew we couldn't go back in
to face your mother like that; if I didn't see you
lose your shoe, what other dangers might I have missed?

Show me the shoe, I ordered. Where
did you leave your shoe?
Happily, you pointed a chubby finger and led me
clambering over logs among bushes along the fringe of a
                                        wetland
Shoe! you cried, triumphantly. *Shoe! Shoe!*
The birds took flight at your exhortations.
Your finger poked the air at angry yellowjackets
anxious frogs indifferent worms frightened beetles
under rotten logs *Shoe! Shoe!* you preached
unabashedly, patient to the verge of tears
until finally, discouraged
that I just didn't get it,
me defeated, angry, sweating, humiliated,
not quite yet deflected by your punnish humour,
unable to fathom
this unbridled curiosity
unable to understand the real meaning of shoe,
you guided me gently back home.

Five years later on the Bruce Trail
along the Niagara Escarpment

on a family hike, Sunday exercise,
knowing that legs can be
exercised any time,
you exercised your prerogative
to slow us down
to uncover beetles under rocks, bright yellow mushrooms
on trees, a snake suddenly dancing in your hand.
Don't worry Dad it's not poisonous ...
just has anticoagulant; you just bleed. I read
about it in the book on snakes and reptiles.
I was beginning to be okay with this,
even as a father,
until, a couple of years later
you tried the same trick in Java,
brushing between green leafy things
to snatch at a snake, me falling for your bluff
(it was a bluff, wasn't it?) pulling you back,
stiff with fear as I watched the snake-head
skim over the ditchwater away.
Even I had read some books about
tropical snakes; this was not Ontario;
I was not born yesterday.

And now, nineteen,
playing Celtic music on an open stage,
silhouetted against the summer afternoon sun,
you reach into that jungle of worried confusion
we surround our children with,
into the darkness of our hidden fears,
pull out your flute,
like a silver tree-snake.
In the branches of your arms it transforms,
the notes bending slightly in the wind,
piping from the dense thicket of you,
from the light pattering between leaves,
from the long-haired willow of your body
like a bird, chuckling
puckishly after rain.

You are Not a Cat
a father's advice to his children

Make friends. Challenge them. Wait for them.
Let your friends go. Make new ones. Welcome the old ones
back. Stand by them. Sit by them.
Worry with them. Think of something bigger
of which you are a part. Create a community. Enlarge it.
Make a place for wasps, walnut trees and grackles.
Include Germany, Jordan, Belize, Indonesia
and Davis Inlet. Listen to everything
around you.

Grow up. Laugh about it. Love your innocence.
Nurture it. Love your experience. Be complicated.
Live simply. Play. Be amazed. Doubt.
When in doubt, trust.
When trust is betrayed, doubt
and trust again.
Be disillusioned.

If you are a cat, be a cat.
If you are an ant, be an ant.
If you got through grade one, get real:
you are neither cat nor insect.
Dig a compost hole.
Sit with the cat, watching ants and squirrels.
Water the roses.
Listen for worms with the robins.

Have strong opinions. Argue.
Change your mind.
Make enemies. Love your enemies.
Fight for their rights. Demand your responsibilities.
Relax. Let go.

Never forget. Always forgive.
If you can't remember, let it go:

if it needs you, it will
come back.

Let the buck stop with you.
If you have a buck, share it.
Read books.
Talk to your father. Listen
to your mother. Feel
the wind on your face. Feel
the waters around you. Rise up.
Pray without ceasing.

When your cat dies,
cry your heart out.
Return your heart to its proper place.
Do an autopsy to see why
the cat died.
Remember this for your next cat.
Bury her in the back yard.
Plant a rose bush over her.
Prune the bush.
Pile cow manure around it.
Relish the scent.
Cultivate your powers of observation.
Look again.

Lose a good argument.
Be devastated.
Do good. Do it well.
Succeed. Fail. Grow.

Use e-mail. Write. Call.
Keep secrets. Share them over tea
with muffins. Be a character
in many others' lives.
Think in stories. Talk in parables.
Hum to yourself.
Sing with your friends.

Drop by for no reason.
If we are not in,
drop a note in the mailbox.

Just say hi.

Dinner-time

One morning after 25 years
of wandering about
halls, stairs, rooms, forests, gardens,
thinking I know us pretty well,
I lean up into the stairwell
to call the kids for supper

and there is a path into a ravine,
snakes slipping past rocks
into a cave, a rattle in the air,
an orange, like an egg in a nest of daffodils,
a vista of apparently impassable mountains,
a large black bear, licking honey from her paws
beside the rush of water over stone.
How could I have missed this?
Did it just appear?
How can I be sure?
I slide down to my haunches,
back against a rock wall,
orange like a baseball in my hand,
then right down, with a sigh,
my feet dangling over a sharp drop-away:
the stairs down to the kitchen.
Mist rises from below.
The borscht is boiling.
I peel the orange,
quelling that old fear of heights,
the fear of my desire to leap
with a glee-full scream off cliffs,
and buildings, sun on my face,
heart pounding, mind racing,
knowing everything, finally,
all at once.

How shall I ever know you?
Is 50 years enough? A lifetime?
The bear waves her head, slowly,

side to side. With my teeth, I pull
a juicy piece of orange
away from its peel.

Downstairs, dinner is waiting.

Half Century Poem

When you are a child
in Winnipeg
running between snowbanks,
invisible snow puppies
tumble curly-tailed after you
squeaking like rubber boots
at 40 below,
nipping at your heels
between the up-pull of your long-johns
and down-tug of your socks.

Your socks are searching for a warm spot
at the toe of your boot.
Like you escaping
your genes
your heritage
your parents
it's all nip and tug
just to find a small dark
boot-toe where you
can sag
without guilt.

Your parents are
like adolescent sheep dogs
keeping you, almost,
on the straight
and slippery
sidewalk.

At twenty you sprint free,
your lungs biting the blue air,
the air biting back.
The puppies flop wearily;
you forget them;
you laugh.

At forty you are so engrossed
in perfecting the brush strokes

of the life you will create,
this work of art
in shades of ochre and forest green,
the still pond in the middle,
the picture of you,
pulling yourself up
by your own bootstraps,
hoisting with your own petard,

you do not see the shadows
gathering themselves,
trying out their various shapes,
the possibilities of revenge or blessing,
in flickering candle-light
at your back.

One wintry day at fifty you are out,
not quite jogging,
not that righteous, walking briskly
to the video store;
you hear a noise
in the dusk behind you.

Turning, it takes a moment
for your eyes to adjust
to the jumble of Christmas lights,
cars, houses, trees, roads not taken,
wet gusts of snow, all that wistful
mumbo-jumbo of dids and might have beens:
startled, your heart leaps at the sudden yellow eyes
of the big black Newfoundland dog
unstoppable, already tumbling over you: your life,
what you have made of it
while you weren't looking.

It knocks you over
all tongue, wet breath, good-hearted
beastliness, holding you
down on the cold snow-patchy grass

so doggily pleased
at having saved you
from the wild cold crashing sea of yourself.

Somewhere in your head
words are taking shape,
some way to articulate
this wonderful strangeness
you have become,
words like fish breaking the surface
of your mind

like invisible puppies
in the wintry air
tumbling, on another sidewalk
in another part of town,
after your kids.

Rebecca
for high school graduation

Somehow it all comes back to dancing.

The old Mennonite Brethren teaching
that dancing is forbidden
because it leads to sex
is only partly right. Another step in the circle
and sex leads to babies.

Just another little animal
getting born, I said. I'm a veterinarian.
I can handle this.
Good thing the doctor arrived,
in an airplane, out of the blue southern skies,
just in time.
From the spirit of your Opa,
one month dead and still telling stories,
from the sun dogs dancing up a dazzle
in the bright prairie sky,
out of the lung-busting cold of that northern winter
you came, a bundle of screaming
sunshine.

And then, who would have thought it,
a circle is completed
and babies lead to dancing.

And then we had Oma's meat buns.
And Matthew welcomed you with a toy,
after which he asked
when you were going home.

It is the duty of children
to teach and test their parents,
and to frighten them,
in equal measure,
tasks you took up
with cheerful energy.

All the long drive from Alberta to Ontario
you cried your four-month-old

lungs out; something about cars
you knew then already,
trying to tell us
how they would call you out
into a street in St. Jacob's,
how in Guelph they would rush through the rain
and bash you.

Another test: the day you tumbled
down the stairs
and held your breath
while Mom and Dad rushed you
frantically to the doctor
and then you sighed,
and held your blanky,
planning no doubt
a run up the stairs
at the CN Tower
to raise money for the World Wildlife Fund.

And when you gave Mr. Fluff, that venerable
stuffed dog, to Matthew, you taught us
a lesson in community-building –
to get what you really want
you must give it away
and then share it back.

On the Bruce Trail, you always ran ahead
along the cliffs, dancing in and out
of sunlight, eager to see
where it all led.
But when you dance too close
to life's dark edge,
sometimes a hand reaches
from the darkness, wanting to touch you.

You and Kathy were playing in the low surf
on Java's south coast.
I was on the cliffs above, exploring,

when I heard below the muffled roar
of a rogue wave from the south pole,
blindly grasping at the half-seen glittery
bits of life. Neptune roared,
I want those!
Matthew clambered up the rocks,
you disappeared
and Kathy reached, caught your tiny hand
and held: a mother's love stronger,
this time, than the blind
and hungry sea-mouthed earth,

whose retreating fingers,
rasping over sand and rocks,
left scars of love and fear across our hearts.

But, having once reached for you,
and slipped off empty handed,
the earth could not flee fast enough before the logic
of Mr. Fluff, as with a magic
Balinese-dance tilt of the head, you held
and pulled it back
and embraced it to yourself.
From the Spice Islands to Germany,
from Clearbrook to Calcutta to China
Elkhart to Kitchener,
the earth sprawls across your bed,
telling stories,
filling you with her voices,
the voices of children and old women,
cats and waves
and the silence in trees,
until, sometimes, your heart cannot bear it.

It clenches, like a flower at dusk,
like your temper at the breakfast table,

and you are dancing again
spinning bright and dark threads
from tears and laughing,
sewing a hem on the chaos,
skirting the darkness with piano duets,
violin-tunes behind the old furnace,
choir songs and ratty stuffed dogs and poetry,
and fresh chocolate chip cookies,

until your heart, made empty
by all the small things, all the little
cookies of day to day,
softens like a hand unfolding,

each new day's tiny animal,
stirring with dreams,
asleep in its palm.

Coyotes at Eyebrow Lake, Saskatchewan

Like a silent, solemn, wire-haired choir,
the coyotes file in
along the coulee's moonlit rim,
awaiting the conductor's whim
to set their voices, held like anxious birds
in slender cages, free.
The poet sinks into the sleepy, self-indulgent
dusk of his tent, unaware.
Eyebrow Lake winks,
flashing a half-moon.
The orgasmic hoot and holler
of the sudden coyote hootenany,
an extended, happy, off-key
full-hearted family campfire song,
breaks over the valley.
The poet scrambles for unidentified
feelings, missing words,
superlatives lost among the musty pile
of socks and two-day underwear.
Sand Hill Cranes lift,
wing on wing, soft, coughing purrs
against the night.
The poet sits, stunned,
amid the litter of his daily rhyme,
terrified by sudden fleeting joy.

Notes

1. *Love and Chaos.* One of the parables
   told by scientific researchers into chaos
   theory is that, under certain conditions,
   in nonlinear systems, a butterfly, flapping
   its wings in the Amazon rain forest
   might initiate a series of events resulting
   in a hurricane over Chicago several days
   later.

2. *Concatenations.* Cats seldom have written
   names. This one was called Gato, which
   is Spanish for cat, and Gateau, which is
   French for cake, because she came on
   Kathy's birthday. A Venezuelan friend
   pointed out that she should be Gata,
   being a female, but this would only be
   confusing for the cat.

3. *For Mother: Weinachtswuensch 1995.*
   A Weinachtswuensch is a poem, song
   recitation or the like that family members
   might contribute to a Christmas Eve
   gathering. To make röllche, you roll out a
   rectangle of pie pastry, spoon pie filling
   down the middle, and fold over the
   pastry, making a long roll.

Acknowledgements

Many of these poems were written for particular people, and read at specific occasions (birthdays, graduations, anniversaries, weddings, workshops on complexity, conferences, etc). The people who received those poems know who they are, and, with a few exceptions, I have chosen not to distract the reader with their names. Not sure if a particular poem was written for you? If the poem fits, wear it. Several of these poems have been accepted by, published in, or read on, the C.B.C. Radio (Morningside), *Fiddlehead*, *Grain*, *Kairos*, *Preventive Veterinary Medicine* and *In Newer Veins: an Anthology of Poetry Written by Veterinary Surgeons*, A.R. Michell and E. Boden eds. (Primrose Hill Press, London, England, 1998).

Special thanks to Stan Dragland, for helping to keep me in tune.

About the Author

David Waltner-Toews lives in Kitchener, Ontario. A veterinary epidemiologist, he teaches at the University of Guelph and consults on environmental matters over much of the world. He has published six books of poetry, including this one, and two volumes of essays.